READ
=ME=
POETRY

D0265892

Don't Hit Your Sister
And Other Family Poems

Acknowledgements

Every effort has been made to obtain permission to reproduce copyright material but there may be cases where we have been unable to trace a copyright holder. The publisher apologizes for any such error and will be happy to correct any omission in future printings.

"Brother" by Mary Ann Hoberman. © 1959, renewed 1987, 1998 Mary Ann Hoberman. Reprinted by permission of Gina Maccoby Literary Agency

"Fair's Fair" © June Crebbin. Reprinted by permission of the author

"The Quarrel" © Eleanor Farjeon from SILVER SAND AND SNOW published by Michael Joseph. Reprinted by permission of David Higham Associates

"Don't Hit Your Sister" © Lesley Miranda. Reprinted by permission of the author

"Conker Collectors" from COWS MOO, CARS TOOT! by June Crebbin. © 1995 June Crebbin, published by Viking

"Buttering" and "Itch" by Roger McGough. © 1990 Roger McGough. Reprinted by permission of PFD on behalf of Roger McGough

"My Sister Laura" © Spike Milligan. Reprinted by permission of Spike Milligan Productions

"Last Word" and "Don't" from DON'T PUT MUSTARD IN THE CUSTARD. © 1985 Michael Rosen. Reprinted by permission of PFD on behalf of Michael Rosen

"Children, Children" (p.12) © Roy Benjamin. Reprinted by permission of Benjamin-Taylor Associates

"Will You Wear the Checked Dress?" from WHO DREW ON BABY'S HEAD? by Michael Rosen. © 1991 Michael Rosen. Reprinted by permission of PFD on behalf of Michael Rosen

"My Kite" from COWS MOO, CARS TOOT! by June Crebbin. © 1995 June Crebbin, published by Viking

"Tea with Aunty Mabel", "Polishing Grandad" and "The Face Inside the Frame" © Jeanne Willis, from TOFFEE POCKETS published by Bodley Head. Reprinted by permission of Random House, UK

"Goodbye Granny" © Pauline Stewart from SINGING DOWN THE BREADFRUIT AND OTHER POEMS published by Red Fox. Reprinted by permission of Random House, UK

"Grandpa" by Berlie Doherty from WALKING ON AIR published by Hodder 1999. Reprinted by permission of David Higham Associates

For Tayte with much love
A. B.

First published 2001 by Walker Books Ltd
87 Vauxhall Walk, London SE11 5HJ

2 4 6 8 10 9 7 5 3 1

This selection © 2001 CLPE/LB Southwark
Individual poems © as noted in acknowledgements
Illustrations © 2001 Ailie Busby

This book has been typeset in Adobe Caslon

Printed in Singapore

British Library Cataloguing in Publication Data:
a catalogue record for this book is
available from the British Library

ISBN 0-7445-6882-X

Don't Hit Your Sister
And Other Family Poems

Selected by Myra Barrs and Sue Ellis

Illustrated by Ailie Busby

WALKER BOOKS
AND SUBSIDIARIES
LONDON • BOSTON • SYDNEY

BROTHER

I had a little brother
And I brought him to my mother
And I said I want another
Little brother for a change.
But she said don't be a bother
So I took him to my father
And I said this little bother
Of a brother's very strange.

But he said one little brother
Is exactly like another
And every little brother
Misbehaves a bit he said.
So I took the little bother
From my mother and my father
And I put the little bother
Of a brother back to bed.

Mary Ann Hoberman

FAIR'S FAIR

When my little sister
Comes into my room,
I tell her to go.

"No," she says.
"I don't have to."

"If you don't," I say,
"I'll tell Mum."

"It's a free world," she says.

"Well, if it's a free world,
I'll go and play in your room."

It always works.

"It's not fair," she shouts,
As she stamps out.

June Crebbin

THE QUARREL

I quarrelled with my brother
I don't know what about,
One thing led to another
And somehow we fell out.
The start of it was slight,
The end of it was strong,
He said he was right,
I knew he was wrong!

We hated one another.
The afternoon turned black.
Then suddenly my brother
Thumped me on the back,
And said, "Oh, *come* along!
We can't go on all night –
I was in the wrong."
So he was in the right.

Eleanor Farjeon

DON'T HIT YOUR SISTER

He hit me on the face, Mummy
so I hit him back

He hit me on the leg, Mummy
so I hit him back

He hit me on the back, Mummy
so I hit him back on the back

He hurlded me, Mummy
so I hurlded him back

He was the one who started it, Mummy
so I started it back.

Lesley Miranda

CONKER COLLECTORS

Every autumn
my brother and I
shuffle through leaves
looking for conkers.

He bakes his in the oven,
soaks them in vinegar,
threads them on a string
and bashes them.

But I pile mine up
on the windowsill
and just look.

June Crebbin

BUTTERING

When my little sister
wants something
she butters up my dad.

If she doesn't get it
she scrapes it all off
HARD!

Roger McGough

My Sister Laura

My sister Laura's bigger than me
And lifts me up quite easily
I can't lift her, I've tried and tried;
She must have something heavy inside.

Spike Milligan

Itch

My sister had an itch
I asked if it was catching.
"Catch," she said, and threw it.
Now I'm the one who's scratching.

Roger McGough

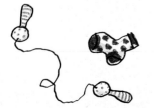

LAST WORD

Dad says:
Stop doing that:
So the boy stuck his tongue out.
Dad says:
Don't stick your tongue out at me.
So the boy says:
I'm not. I'm just licking my lips.

Later:
BANG BANG BANG BANG.
Dad says:
Stop jumping up and down up there
I can't stand the noise.
And the girl says:
I'm not jumping. I'm hopping.
Dad says:

Some people always get the last word.

Michael Rosen

CHILDREN, CHILDREN

Children, children.
Yes, Mama?
Where did you went to?
To see Granpa.
What did he give you?
Bread and patata.
Where did you put it?
Upon de ledge.
Suppose it drop.
I don't give a rap.

Traditional

CHILDREN, CHILDREN

Children, children.
Yes, Papa?
Where have you been to?
Grand-mamma.
What did she give you?
Bread and jam.
Where is my share?
Up in the air.
How can I reach it?
Climb on a chair.
Suppose I fall?
I don't care!

Traditional

MOM AND ME ONLY

Some kids at school have a mom and a dad.

I've got Mom and me only.

On Parents' Night it makes me mad

that it's Mom and me only.

"You've got it good," Danitra says when I am sad.

"Your mama loves you twice as much. Is that so bad?"

Danitra knows just what to say to make me glad.

With her around, I'm never lonely.

Nikki Grimes

WILL YOU WEAR THE CHECKED DRESS?

Will you wear the checked dress today?
But Mum says not today.

So I wait three days
and then I say,
Will you wear the checked dress today?
And she says,
Yes I will today.

And I like it all day.

Michael Rosen

MY KITE

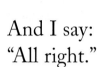

On windy days
my dad says:
"Let's fly your kite."

And I say:
"All right."

So we go up the hill
behind our house
and Dad unravels the string
S L O W L Y
while I walk backwards
S L O W L Y
holding the kite.

Then Dad says: "Right,
let go."

So I do,
and usually the kite
goes straight up in the air.

Now I'm not saying Dad isn't good.
He can make the kite do anything,
twist and turn, dip and dive,
a hundred different ways.

"Isn't this fun?" Dad says.
"Just look at it go."

I know.

It's just that I wish,
sometimes,
he'd let me have a go.

June Crebbin

DON'T

Don't do,
Don't do,
Don't do that.
Don't pull faces,
Don't tease the cat.

Don't pick your ears,
Don't be rude at school.
Who do they think I am?

Some kind of fool?

One day
they'll say
Don't put toffee in my coffee
don't pour gravy on the baby
don't put beer in his ear
don't stick your toes up his nose.
Don't put confetti on the spaghetti
and don't squash peas on your knees.

Don't put ants in your pants
don't put mustard in the custard

don't chuck jelly at the telly

and don't throw fruit at the computer
don't throw fruit at the computer.

Don't what?
Don't throw fruit at the computer.
Don't what?
Don't throw fruit at the computer.
Who do they think I am?
Some kind of fool?

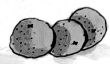

Michael Rosen

TEA WITH AUNTY MABEL

If you ever go to tea with my Aunty Mabel,

Never put your elbows on the dining-room table,

Always wipe your shoes if you've been in the garden,

Don't ever burp. If you do, say pardon.

Don't put your feet on the new settee,

If she offers you a sugar lump, don't take three.

Don't dunk your biscuits, don't make crumbs,

Don't bite nails and don't suck thumbs.

Don't rock the budgie, don't tease the peke,

Speak when you're spoken to or else don't speak.

Do as you're told and if you're not able,

Don't go to tea with my Aunty Mabel.

Jeanne Willis

EARS COCKED

There's five of us in the family,

But only one who gobbles like mad

And grabs his coat at the sound of a train:

    That's Dad.

There's one who hears the smallest sneeze

And the other tell-tale sounds that come

From the cot upstairs or the pram outside:

    That's Mum.

A hoot, a whistle and a hoot again

To three of us mean nothing at all;

To two they mean, "Hi, come and play":

    Me and Paul.

The cracked tin voice of the ice-cream van

On Saturdays, just when tea is done,

Brings the lot of us tumbling through the door –

    Bar one.

Raymond O'Malley

GOODBYE GRANNY

Goodbye Granny
it's nearly time to fly
goodbye Granny
I am going in the sky.
I have my suitcase
and things.
You have packed
me everything
except the sunshine.
All our good times
are stored
up inside
more than enough
for any plane ride.
Goodbye Granny
things will be all right
goodbye Granny
I won't forget to write.
Goodbye Granny
bye! bye!
bye! bye!

Pauline Stewart

GRANDPA

Grandpa's hands are as rough as garden sacks

And as warm as pockets.

His skin is crushed paper round his eyes

Wrapping up their secrets.

Berlie Doherty

POLISHING GRANDAD

Grandad's got no hair.

He's got a shiny head.

Because there's nothing

There to brush,

I polish him instead.

Jeanne Willis

THE FACE INSIDE THE FRAME

Grandad's got a photograph
Of him when he was small,
It doesn't really look like Grandad
Very much at all.
But Chrissie said that she was sure
The face inside the frame
Was Grandad's, and she pointed out
His smile was just the same.

Jeanne Willis

OTHER READ ME BOOKS

Read Me Beginners are simple rhymes and stories ideal for children learning to read.

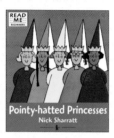

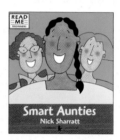

Read Me Story Plays are dramatized versions of favourite stories, written for four or more voices to share.